Accelerated Learning

Master Memory Improvement, Be Productive and Declutter Your Mind To Boost Your IQ Through Insane Focus, Unlimited Memory, Photographic Memory, Speed Reading, and Mindfulness

Adam Hunter

Table of Contents

consent and can in no way be considered an endorsement from the trademark holder.

Introduction

Memory and learning, as I'm sure you know, are important to everything you do in life. That's why you are here. The information you are going to learn can be helpful in many different areas of life. You can use this information to help you learn a new language, learn new things in a shorter time period, prepare for a test, remember names, and a whole host of things. The key is tapping into your memory.

Centuries ago, our ancestors saw memorization as a prized skill. They passed cultures down through the years by remembering laws, taboos, history, legends, and stories. Then, when the printing press was created, people started to "look things up," instead of remembering them. Today, we have Google and the internet, which is pretty much preventing us from using our memory. What we can't remember, all we have to do is look it up.

Teachers don't require their students to memorize multiplication tables, famous speeches, poems, and many other types of academic material as often today. These things used to be ingrained in students' minds. The disdain for memorization grew along with other intellectually damaging effects of the post-modern world. Now, education focuses on hands-on activities, inquiry learning, critical thinking, new math, among other things. These new emphases are important, except they don't allow children to learn how to memorize things. This has created mentally lazy people. This is no fault of their own, it just happened. This can be remedied and should be because mental laziness isn't going to allow you to succeed.

Memorization disciplines your mind. When you have a lazy mind, it can cause you to be easily distracted, think very little about things, or you think in a sloppy manner. Memorization will train your mind to be industrious and remain focused.

There will be times where you can't just "Google it." You may not have access to the internet, or your phone could be dead. Not everything is available on the internet, either. There is a great deal of irrelevant information that you will find when you search for things as well. There are also times when looking things up isn't helpful in certain situations, like when you are learning to use a foreign language, when you are asked to make an impromptu speech, or when you want to be an expert on a subject.

Memorization will also create the things that we think about. Nobody is able to think when they are in a vacuum of information. In order to be an expert on anything, you have to have knowledge about it.

People think using the ideas that working memory holds onto, which is only able to be accessed quickly from their stored memory. Understanding things is improved by the information that you have in your working memory. Without this kind of knowledge, you will experience a mind full of mush.

The muscles that you use when you memorize things develop learning and improve your ability to learn. The more that you are able to remember, the more you will be able to learn.

History shows us that great minds and full of knowledge. Picasso had to have an understanding of how to paint before you picked up a brush and began to paint something. Einstein had to have a good understanding of the physics of his time before he was able to see the errors within it. Plato had to have a good understanding of Greek philosophy before he was able to find his Academy in North Athens. Steve Jobs had to have a good understanding of programming before he created Apple.

If you are interested in learning more, you have to go back to the basics that have worked for people in the past. What people have been doing isn't working. The fundamental skill that people forget about is memorization.

Memorization is only the start of accelerated learning, though. The next important thing is focus. Focus and memory work hand in hand. You can't memorize things if you aren't focused, and you can't focus on something unless you are able to access memorized information.

But why is focus so important? When you are focused on one thing for a certain time period you will do better work, get more done quicker, and your creativity will be improved. Staying focused on one thing at a time is also less stressful on your mind. When you are less stressed, you will be happier.

To be focused means that you have created clear goals and objectives. You work towards reaching those goals and objectives. When you try to figure out what you are going to do, you base your decision on what you need to do in order to progress towards your goals with the resources and time that you have available.

When you are focused on the present, you are only focused on the activity that you need to complete. Anything else that is going on isn't important, so you remove distractions so that you give the task at hand you full and undivided attention.

The alternative to being focused is doing a bunch of other things, jumping from task to task without completely finishing something. Those who aren't focused normally spend their time doing anything but what they need to get done. What they choose to do is often dictated by:

- What makes them feel busier

- What feels easier

- Bullies who tell them what to do

- Another person's priorities

- Urgency

Think about multitasking where people believe they are getting a lot done, but they are working slower and at a lower standard. Over and over, research has found that multitasking isn't possible and serves no purpose. Staying focused and finishing a single task at a time before going to something else is more effective.

There are a lot of different reasons why people find it hard to remain focused. One thing is for sure, we live in a world where we are constantly being distracted by social media, internet, cell phones, radio, TV, as well as more people that live closer together.

Not only that, but we live in a consumerist economy. So many different entities depend on us spending more money so that they can make more money. This means that we are faced with more disruptions in the way of billboards, neon signs, mail, phone calls, and emails to push marketing in our face. It's hard to take a quiet stroll in the park without noticing some sort of advertisement.

It's hard to get rid of all of our distractions. The best way to do so is to find a room where you can shut the door and turn off all electronics that you can and turn off notifications, but even still, if you let anybody know where you are, they could easily distract you.

The benefits of being focused are endless. First off, tasks get finished faster than if you are trying to finish two or more things. Let's say you are trying to take an online Spanish course, do your homework for another class, and research information more an upcoming paper. That list sounds stressful; now imagine jumping from task to task. The best thing to do is set everything aside except one of them.

When you turn your attention to one task, you can finish it with fewer mistakes. That means your work is going to be higher quality. Also, your creativity will kick in, which will allow you to come up with new ideas. This is perfect for a person who creates things, like musicians, writers, photographers, artists, as well as, researchers, teachers, or anybody who needs ideas.

When you are constantly connected and have to work through distractions, it will affect your stress levels and productivity. Without focus, you don't get a lot of things done. This will cause you to fall behind, which adds even more stress. It's sometimes hard to figure out what you should be doing and what you shouldn't when you have a lot on your plate. Look at what you need to do. Is there any work that:

- Should be automated

- Should be outsourced

- Should be delegated

- Should be done by another person

- Or, shouldn't be done at all

It's easy to take on too much, which just causes more stress.

When you focus on something, you will use your subconscious mind. Think back to when you learned to ride a bike. At first, it was hard. When you started focusing on the things you were doing, the subconscious took over and help you to learn. This is true for your tasks you do every day. When of focus on one thing, your subconscious will be able to kick in help you finish it.

While you are working on one part of it, your subconscious will work on another part. You will notice when you continue on with a task that you don't have to think about it as much. This is where memory also comes in as well. Your subconscious will only work if you have something memorized about a topic.

It's easy to forget the importance of memory and focus in this day and age. With the information we are going to cover, you will learn how to re-engage your mind to improve your life.

Covering the Basics (Insane Focus)

To really get into unlocking improved learning and memory, you have to understand a few basic things about the mind.

Kill Multi-Tasking

We've already talked about how problematic multitasking is, but studies have even found that it can kill your performance and could end up hurting the brain. A study performed at Stanford University found that multitasking is less productive than focusing on a single task at a time. They also found that those who regularly bombarded their self with streams of outside information aren't able to pay attention, switch between tasks efficiently, or recall information as well as those who work on a single task.

They even went so far as to test those who believe that multitasking is a special skill. They compared groups of people based on how often they multitasked and their belief that it could improve their performance. They discovered that the heavy multitaskers were worse at multitasking than the people who focused on one thing. They performed worse because they could organize their thoughts and filter out things that were irrelevant, and they were slower when it came to switching to a different task.

Research has also found that besides slowing your down, multitasking lowers the IQ. A study at the University of London discovered that people who multitasked while performing cognitive tasks had their IQ scores decline by a similar amount to staying up all night. Men who multitasked had a 15 point drop, placing them in an average range of eight-year-olds.

So, when you find yourself typing up a report while in a business meeting, remember that your cognitive skills are being hurt so much so that you may as well have an eight-year-old write that report for you.

Not only will it affect your IQ, but it could cause permanent cognitive impairment. A study at the University of Sussex compared the time that people spend on multiple devices to MRI brain scans. They discovered that heavy multitaskers had decreased brain density in their anterior cingulate cortex. This is the region of the brain that is responsible for empathy as well as emotional and cognitive control. While there needs to be more research to figure out if multitasking is indeed physically damaging to the brain, it's clear that it has a lot of negative side effects.

If you tend to multitask, it's something that you don't want to indulge in often. Even if it doesn't create permanent brain damage, it will fuel existing difficulties you have with attention to detail, organization, and concentration. Multitasking also indicated low social and self-awareness, which are two emotional intelligence skills that are important for success at work. When you multitask, you are not only harming your performance at that moment; you could be damaging a part of your brain that is important for future success.

Focus on One Thing

Knowing what we know about multitasking, the only other option is to focus on one thing at a time. While there may be some that would still argue that doing more faster is the best path to productivity, I would argue that they're wrong. While you may be busier, you aren't being productive.

The attention we have to give what we need to work on is limited. The mind can only focus on so many things, so we need to invest our attention wisely. Single-tasking is the opposite of multitasking, and it is so much better in every way imaginable. The brain will likely resist this because it isn't as stimulating as multitasking. But when we work on a single task, it allows us to dive deeper and do better work. You won't be forced to spread your time, energy, and attention across several things at one time. Single-tasking creates attentional space around our work. This allows us to think deeper, create connections, work creatively, and find more meaning.

Take a moment to think back to the last time you were crazy-productive. Chances are, you weren't doing a million different things. You were probably working on one thing, and spending all of your energy, time, and attention on that one item. While it is going to take you some energy and time to adapt to being less stimulated during your day, you can easily see why it's worth it.

Single-tasking also increases our "attention muscles." This is how much control we have over our attention. Harvard psychologists Daniel Gillbert and Matthew Killingsworth found that 47% of our waking hours are used thinking about things that are completely unrelated to what is in front of us. The ramifications are huge: a person who is attentive 75% of the time will be more productive than a person who focuses on their work 50% of the time. When we single-task, we build our attention muscles because we have to constantly rein in our attention.

Don't believe me? Try single-tasking for the next week. Set yourself a 20-minute timer, and take that time to focus on a single task. At first, your brain will resist this, but once you get into the groove of it, you will feel amazing. Afterward, think about what you were able to accomplish in 20 minutes.

Productivity and being busy are two unrelated things. Instead, productivity and what you accomplish is what you should look at.

Be Present

With all the work and things going through our minds, it's easy to start feeling stressed and overwhelmed. This is because we are trying to store too much in short-term memory. Multitasking tends to be to blame for this as well. By dumping all of our thoughts and to-do lists into our short-term, we cause an endless information loop that we can't quit thinking about. We constantly feel like we have forgotten something.

It's like we have a hamster in our mind running endlessly on its wheel but getting absolutely nowhere. It causes us to feel physically and mentally exhausted. The mind has an amazing ability to remember unfinished tasks. This is what is called the Zeigarnik Effect. We have a "reminder system" built-in our minds. This can be useful at times, but in our modern world, it doesn't work all that well so we get overloaded. And then we can't get those thoughts out of our mind

The secret to fixing this problem is simple. We have to get this stuff out of our mind. All of those reminders and ideas need to be placed in a reliable system that will watch out for the information until the time comes where we can deal with it all. We need a way to be present at the moment, and make sure that your mind is clear.

The first thing you need to do is capture your thoughts and get them into your systems as quickly as possible. This can be a notebook that you keep with you, or you can use a free app. It doesn't matter what you do, as long as it will be something that you always have with you.

Then you have to create a daily reminder to look over the thoughts that you have captured and figure out what you are going to do. Google Calendar can send you a message on certain times to remind you to do this. When you get the reminder, you will go through the information you wrote down and figure out what you are going to do with the items. You will decide one of four things for each of the items:

- Delete – the item isn't serving any purpose and doesn't need to be done.

- Delegate – somebody else could do this.

- Defer – this can be done later.

- Do – this something I need to finish now.

That's it. When you do this on a regular basis, it will clear out your mind and allow you to focus on the task at hand. You will be more present, and you won't have to deal with your mind clutter anymore.

Imagination

The last basic you need to understand is the power of your imagination. Imagination influences everything we do. It is what creates elaborate inventions, dreams, and theories in every profession. Ultimately, imagination will influence all that we do no matter our profession.

I want you to take a moment and think about how you could use your imagination in a more deliberate and effective manner. How could you improve your personal and professional if you started to use your brain in ways that you haven't ever before?

There is nothing shameful or childish about making imagination as part of your everyday life. The more that you use your imagination, the stronger it will become. You will be amazed as you use your imagination and tap into an amazing source of infinite possibilities.

The one thing that every successful person has in common is how they use their imagination. Take, for example, Bill Gates and Steve Jobs. They imagined how personal computers could change the world, how they work, how it could teach children, and how it could entertain people.

Imagination isn't just helpful when it comes to envisioning the future. It's also helpful when it comes to learning and remembering things. Our sense of sight has evolved to become one of our strongest senses, so it's only natural that our mind likes to see things in order to remember them.

That's why you will find the majority of our memory techniques will use your imagination and mental images. The problem is, people have been conditioned to believe that imagination is inferior to logical reasoning. They think it's something that only children should do.

With these beliefs, it causes potential great ideas and learning abilities to be smothered, stifled, or killed. It also shows a lack of understanding about how important imagination is in human life.

Unlimited Memory

For our bodies to stay healthy, it's important that we exercise. So why do people not apply the same information to their brain? In order for our memory to improve, we have to train the brain, but this isn't something that has to be time-consuming and strenuous like a workout at the gym. Memory champions and psychologist both agree that the key to a better memory is visualization, and the crazier it is, the better.

Mnemonics are memory techniques that make complicated information easier to remember. The ones that tend to work the best are often rather unusual because the strange parts of life normally are more memorable than the boring ones. One study found that people remembered more information when it had a humorous air about it, so when you are looking to memorize something conjure up a rhyme that will cause you to laugh at how crazy the picture is in your mind.

In another study, researchers found that the method of loci was a great way to retain new information. Those who participated in the study that used the memory technique scored higher on the assessment than the ones who didn't. Method of loci is a memory technique with a lot of potential to use the zaniest parts of your imagination. To master this technique, you visualize a location that you are very familiar with, such as your home, and put the information you need to learn in this location. To improve your recall, you can allow your imagination to run wild. This technique is also referred to as a memory palace, which we will talk about a bit more later on.

Use Your Imagination

It really helps if you can fully immerse yourself in your imagination so that you can improve your memory recall. Researchers at the University of Arizona discovered that people could remember a word better if they were told to think about how well it described them. When you visualize information, picture yourself interacting with the place or object. You can also engage your senses so that you can imagine how it tastes, smells, and feels.

Not everybody is born having an amazing memory, but everybody is able to use their imagination in order to train their brain to remember more information they have learned. Boris Konrad and Martin Dresler discovered that mnemonic brain training is something everybody can use to improve their memory, not just those special memory champions. The only thing you need is visualization and imagination.

So, if imagination has such a huge impact on memory, imagine what could happen if you make it a part of your daily habit to improve your imagination? I want you to try this simple activity. This will take less than three minutes and is the perfect way to exercise your visualization ability to allow your imagination to run free.

- Pick an object you have around you – we'll go with your cell phone.

- Now, shut your eyes and take about ten seconds or so to describe how your phone looks.

- Open your eyes and then look at your phone to see if there are any other details that you could have described.

- Close your eyes again, and describe everything that you can remember about your phone.

- Once done, open your eyes again and pick a different object – we'll say it's your laptop.

- Now, you are going to engage your imagination. You want to picture your cell phone interacting with your laptop in some way. Allow this to become crazy. Perhaps, your phone could have eyes and arms, and it starts to type out a book on your laptop.

- Shut your eyes one last time and describe a little short story in great detail so that you bring this to life in your mind. Remember, you want it to be bizarre and funny.

This is not only a great way to improve your visualization ability, but it will also allow you to work out your imagination. When you see objects in your mind, and you describe how they interact, you create memorable associations that you won't be able to forget.

If you want, you can start doing this every single day to improve your imagination and visualization. Instead of trying to do the complete exercise every day, which could cause you to become burned out, you can turn it into tiny habits. On the first day, you will just do the first step or so. Over a five day period, you will do more steps until you are doing the complete exercise every day. This will then become automatic.

To make sure that you do this every day, you can pick an anchor that will trigger this action. This could be after you finish your breakfast; you pick an object to describe. Once finished, you celebrate in some way.

Create Pictures

Now that you know and understand the importance of imagination when it comes to remembering things, let's look at the first step in remembering what you want. We are going to create mental snapshots of events. This is a great way to remember events in your life as well.

When you engage your full attention on what is presently happening, it will encourage the creation of stronger, clearer memories of important things. A person's ability to remember detailed events is normally not automatically strong. With the use of mental snapshots, you can have better success in creating long-lasting memories. If you despise your episodic memory, don't worry. Instead, you're going to be able to snap a mental picture or two to improve your odds of remembering things.

Creating photo albums, recording a video of an event, or writing it down in your journal are great ways to preserve memories. But you can't always carry around these physical memory aids. A clear mental image that you can instantly recall is a precious commodity. There are two main types of memory, episodic and semantic. Episodic memory is the memory of events and is one type of declarative memory. Semantic memory is the recollection of general knowledge and concepts.

Your episodic memory is made up of memories of emotions, times, and places associated with a certain event that has happened to you. When you think about your high school graduation or what you ate for breakfast, you are using your episodic memory.

There are some people who are able to recall details easily. There are some people who are so good at this; they have what is known as hyperthymesia, or "excessive remembering." This isn't always a good thing, though.

Jill Price is one of the first hyperthymesic. She can recall every little detail of her life since the age of 14. She finds it distracting, exhausting, uncontrollable, and non-stop.

But this memory trick is for those who are burdened by a perfect memory. This is for those who find themselves saying "I don't remember that." This won't require any special tools. All you need is your brain, an intention, eyes, and a couple of steps that a lot like using a camera.

The important thing to remember when creating a mental snapshot is making sure that you are completely focused on what is happening. You could be there and soaking in most of what is going on, but without realizing it, you aren't connected deeply enough with the special moments. To create a mental snapshot, you have to be able to zoom in on the little things. We will use a wedding as an example of a moment that you want to remember forever.

1. Watch the scene with intent. Make sure you keep your head still. Gaze at what is going on with concentration and focus. Tell yourself that it is important that you are able to remember the details of what is going on. Carefully

observe all of the colors of the scene. Look at the position and arrangement of the wedding party. The dresses that the bridesmaids are wearing. The way the room is lit, how the flowers. Really drink in the moment.

2. Slowly blink your eyes. With your eyes focused intently on what you see before you, you will want to click your brain's camera "shutter" by blinking once at half-speed. Basically, you will want to close and open your eyes at half the speed that they normally move. You can even imagine hearing a "click" like you would when taking a picture.

Now, you will want to take a moment to review the picture you just took in your mind's eye. Close your eyes for a second and conjure up the picture in your memory. Take a mental look at the image you just captured. If you find that your picture is a bit fuzzy, open up your eyes and take a harder look at what you were trying to remember, and then take another snapshot.

This can be used when trying to remember just about anything. It could even be helpful when it comes to remembering a grocery list as well.

Intense focus is what is important to come up with permanent and clear mental snapshots. Focus requires mental effort. The more you practice this technique, the clearer and more detailed your images are going to become.

You shouldn't try to take dozens of pictures like you would with a camera. Instead, you should use your max concentration in just a few moments that represent the entire event. For some things, one mental snapshot could be enough.

Your most lucid memories are likely connected with powerful emotions. Events that you connected to peak moments of loss, fear, accomplishment, and joy are recalled more easily and vividly.

The Rule to Remember Anything

When it comes to memorizing things, there are three steps that you can take that will help you to remember anything and everything. First, you will make sure that you engage as many senses as possible, this means sound, smell, touch, sight, and sometimes taste. Second, you will emphasize your mental image you have created with your senses. This means that you will over exaggerate it so that you couldn't possibly forget it. Lastly, you will make it exciting. This means that you will picture your image doing something. Let's look at each of these steps a bit more.

Use Your Senses

While the mental snapshot technique is helpful in remembering things, there are many other mental image techniques that can help you to remember things. There isn't one best technique; the important thing is that you make it as memorable as possible. This means using as many senses as possible.

Have you ever been walking down the street distracted by your own memories and thoughts, and then you caught a whiff of something? A bakery down the street is making cookies, and the smell of the butter, sugar, and eggs takes you back to another time and place.

Instead of walking down the street, you are in your childhood home playing hide and seek outside while your mother is cooking. Everybody experiences where an image, taste, sound, or smell sends then back in time.

The five senses have the ability to clearly evoke memories of the past and free positive emotions like happiness and pleasure, or it can evoke feelings of anger and fear. A song can make you think of a special moment with an important person, or a road trip you have taken with friends. What's around you can transport you back to the memories of your teens and what you experienced at a certain place.

Of your five senses, the mind may like thinking in pictures, but the sense of smell is the strongest when it comes to evoking memories. A simple scent can unleash a rush of emotions. The smell of perfume, wet grass, or the aroma of coffee can cause you to experience various emotions.

1. Use Smell

When you create a mental image, make sure that you try to use your sense of smell. Smell is most closely connected with your hippocampus, which a brain structure that is responsible for your memory. Smell is also connected with the limbic system, which the emotional area of your brain. All the other senses have to move along a path to reach the areas of the brain that control our emotions and memories.

This is the reason why smell will often awaken vivid memories and bring up sensations that mix sadness and sensitivity, which often called nostalgia. One study performed by Silvia Alava, psychologist, found that people were able to remember 35% of what they smell and around 5% of what they see.

The study explained that when a person smells perfume, it is not only registered in the brain, but it is also associated with an emotion that you are feeling in that moment. When you smell that perfume again, you will experience the emotions again.

2. Use Sight

All of your mental pictures are going to use sight because you can visualize them. As far as sight bringing up memories, a picture of a landscape, bedroom, or object can bring up a moment in your life that you enjoyed. There can also be moments where we feel as if we have experienced a moment before, known as déjà vu.

There are two theories for the experience of déjà vu. One theory explains that when you register an event in your memory, there are parts of the brain that registers things slower than the others, and déjà vu happens when the last parts of the brain process the event. The other theory suggests that sometimes an event create a delay of memories that we have a real or imaginary relationship with the memory.

3. Use Taste

This sense may be a bit hard to use in a memory technique, but if you can figure out how to add in taste, great. When we eat something, the brain will use the sensations of taste with the information that you have stored in your memory, and it will look for data concerning certain things that you can relate with the taste, previous situations, or other types of foods that have had similar stimuli.

4. Use Hearing

Next, you will want to add sound to your mental images. Everybody has, at some point, created a mental soundtrack from songs they have listened to. Our life doesn't come with a spontaneous soundtrack, but a lot of memories will be triggered by a familiar piece of music.

5. Use Touch

Lastly, you want to try to use touch in your mental image as well. Of the five senses, touch is the weakest one. Most of the time, one of your other senses will trigger a memory before you have to use the sense of touch. That said. You can still use touch in your mental picture so that you can be sure that something will trigger your memory.

Create Emphasis

Now that you know that you need to use all of your sense to create a vivid memory, let's look at creating a mental image with emphasis that you won't be able to forget.

To create a strong mental connection with new information, you have to make sure that your images are memorable because it's too easy to forget ordinary things. It's easy to remember the outrageous, the impossible, and the silly. Do you remember what you ate for dinner on Monday three weeks ago?

More than likely not. But, I bet you remember your first day of high school or your first date because these are all memorable events. When it stands out, you are more likely to remember it.

That means you need to make sure that your mental images stand out in some way. Here are a few things to remember when it comes to making memorable images:

- Substitute one item with a different item.

- Has the image come alive?

- Exaggerate the amount of something, which means picture a million of whatever you need to remember.

- Exaggerate a proportion of the item. This could mean that the item is huge in your mind, or only a part of it is large, kind of like a caricature.

Maybe you want to remember that the capital of Peru is Lima. Lima sounds like a lemur, so you could picture a giant lemur swinging around on a tree.

Create Action

The last thing you need to do is bring your mental image to life. Think about when you try to remember a phone number. You might find that you move your fingers in order to help you remember the number. The movement helps you remember something, so when you make your mental image move, you will be able to remember it more easily.

Think back to the mental image of the lemur swinging on the trees. The image had movement; it was alive. Now, this can also be even funnier. Let's look at another mental image to remember the capital of a country. For this one, we will use Montevideo. It is the capital of Uruguay. Now, to me, Montevideo sounds like movie video.

To add movement and to make it crazy, we could picture a large VHS tape (remember those?) take their little VHS family to see a new movie. That's an image you are likely not to forget. And, to wrap things up and connect everything, in this image of the VHS tape family going to the movies, we could add in some other senses. You can imagine the smell of the popcorn of a movie

25

theatre and the sticky feel of the movie theatre floor. See how this all comes together to create something you will always remember? I'll bet you won't forget that Uruguay's capital is Montevideo.

Photographic Memory

The next thing we are going to look at is different ways to create a photographic memory. This means that you will be able to remember different things, like names, places, numbers, and words, in great detail. The photographic memory that most people refer to means that people remember things without the use of mnemonic devices. We are going to use mnemonic devices to create a photographic memory of sorts.

People who have amazing skill at memorizing things, like chess players who can best opponents while blindfolded, or card sharks who can memorize the order of a shuffled deck of cards are typically only good at one task. They can memorize the one thing they are good at. You don't want that, do you? You want to be able to memorize anything and everything that you see or hear, right? That's what we are going to learn to do.

Pages, Words, and Lists

Through evolution, the brain has become great at dealing with sensory information. Through correctly interpreting the five senses, the mind is able to understand the environment. Sight has become the most developed of the human senses. This is why the brain has become extremely good at processing and storing images; especially when they are concrete and real-world objects. Trying to remember abstract symbols, like printed words, is inefficient and unnatural. Words are great ways to communicate, but they aren't the best way for our brain to process information.

Imagery, as you know, is the real language of the mind. Images are the vocab of the mind and the building blocks of any language. When I tell you to think about a horse, what is first the thing that comes to mind? Is it the sequence of letters, H-O-R-S-E? Of course not. The first thing you think of is the picture of a horse; you might even be able to tell me what color it is. Aren't dreams always in images? Pictures are how the mind talks to you, and we need to use that.

To complete understanding the effect that images have for memorizing things, let's take a look at your first memorization technique known as memory pegging. This is a fun little technique and is a great way to memorize words and lists. This is based on thinking in pictures, which you will soon realize most memory techniques will require you to do so.

Before we dive into the technique, I'm going to give you a bit of a challenge. I want you to memorize a list of ten items. You can write this down and study them for about two minutes and then put away the list and don't look at it again. Here is the list:

1. Sausage
2. Eggs
3. Beer
4. Tape
5. Chewing gum
6. Milk
7. Stamps
8. Kale
9. Espresso
10. Tomato

Just like when you learn a new language, you will need to learn basic vocabulary first. We're going to start with some useful words: the numbers one through ten. When you bring the numbers to your visual language, you will be able to use the numbers to memorize your list of words.

There are lots of different ways to change the numbers into images. The best way to do this is to use images that resemble the shape of the numbers. When you remove the abstract symbols of the numbers and replace them with a vivid and colorful image, you will get a better mental picture. Here are a few suggestions:

1. Straw

2. Clothes hanger

3. Lips

4. Kite

5. Chair

6. Croquet mallet

7. Hockey stick

8. Snake

9. Tennis racket

10. Bat and a ball

You can use whatever you feel like you will be able to remember more easily. Once you have created your list of images, take a few images to familiarize yourself with them. These are what will become your pegs, and, once you have learned them, you will be able to use them over and over so that you can memorize everything.

Now that you have your initial vocabulary of images, you will be able to memorize new ones by creating associations between them. All you have to do is combine both images and create a new image. Now you have to use your imagination, remember what we talked about earlier? There is one rule when you do this; it has to be outrageous.

You want it to be as nonsensical, animated, extraordinary, unusual, offensive, ridiculous, and crazy. You want to remember these things, right? Think about what we talked about in the last chapter. The crazier, the better. If it is boring, you are doing it wrong.

If we think back to our grocery list, how can we connect sausage with a straw? You could start by picturing yourself trying to eat a piece of sausage by sucking it up through a straw. If you are able to use your other senses, great, and you can add more imagery to the scene. Think about how hard it would be to try and suck a cooked piece of sausage up through a straw and the force at which you would have to suck. That's going to start hurting, right?

Let's do this again with the second item on the list. We have eggs and a clothes hanger. This one will likely get pretty crazy. You could imagine a row of eggs sitting on the clothes hanger or any other crazy picture that you can think of.

I'm sure by now you get the idea. When you first do this, it can seem like a lot of work to go through each item, but it's not. This action will eventually become automatic, and it's fun.

When you have to recall the list, there's really not much you have to do. The recall will be automatic. All you have to do is ask yourself what the first item is. For number one, you see the straw, and immediately, you see yourself trying to suck sausage up through the straw.

Now, I want you to try to write down the grocery list from earlier in the same order without looking at it. Give yourself a point for each correct word and another point if it was in the correct place. How did you do? The majority of people will get 12 out of 20. If they were asked again a week later without knowing they would be, they would get an abysmal five.

When the pegging method is used, the results are mind-blowing. They typically get a perfect 20, and it normally remains consistent when asked a week later. This is true even when they use the method for the first time.

Link and Story

The next methods we are going to look at are the link and story methods. These are great methods when it comes to remembering lists. The link method is one of the easiest memory devices out there. It helps by creating simple associations between items that are on a list, linking them with a vivid image that holds that item.

You then take the first image and create a connection between it and the next item on your list. You could do this by smashing them together in your mind, place one on top of the other, or so on. You continue through your list in the same manner, linking each item to the next.

The story method works much in the same way, linking each item together with some memorable story feature. The way the story flows and the strength of your images will provide you with cues to retrieval the list.

It is possible for a person to remember a list of words through association only, but, it normally works best when you attach the association to a story. Otherwise, if you forget one association, you could end up forgetting the rest of your list.

Given how fluid this device is, it's important that the images you create are as vivid as you can possibly make them. Let's take a look at how you can use the link and story method to remember a list of towns. The list is Belfast, Derry, Lisburn, Strabane, Downpatrick, Greenisland, Bangor, Newry, and Larne.

Using the link method:

This will use a series of images coding the information:

- A BELl (Belfast) rang down at the DAIRY (Derry) farm.

- The DAIRY farm was BURNing (Lisburn) to the ground.

- This caused the STRAy (Strabane) dog to leave is hiding place.

- PATRICK ran DOWN (Downpatrick) to the fire to help the STRAy dog.

- PATRICK says that the only thing left was a GREEN ISLAND (Greenisland).

- The GREEN ISLAND had a few BANGs (Bangor) and dents in it.

- Besides the BANGs, it was good as NEW (Newry).

- The almost NEW island was used in the LAuNdRy (Larne) as a reminder of the dairy.

There doesn't have to be a point or some reason for the sequence of your images. There just needs to be some link between each so that you can remember the next.

Belfast, Derry, Lisburn, Strabane, Downpatrick, Greenisland, Bangor, Newry, and Larne

Using the story method:

Instead of creating a list of images, you could create an image of the list by creating a vivid story.

The worker rang the BELl FAST (Belfast) to get the attention of the DAIRY (Derry) employees to the fire. The building was BURNing (Lisburn) quickly, but the STRAy (Strabane) dog managed to escape. PATRICK ran DOWN (Downpatrick) the hill to see what he could salvage from the fire. The only thing still standing was a GREEN ISLAND (Greenisland). Besides a few BANGs (Bangor) and dents, the island was good as NEW (Newry). Patrick took the island to the local LAuNdRy (Larne) so that it could be used.

Both of these tools are great ways to remember lists of words. The link method is the most basic technique and easy to create, and the story technique is very similar by linking the words together in a single image.

Acronyms

Another way to remember words or lists are through using acronyms. Acronyms are pretty hard to forget once you have a good one in mind. You can come up with your own for a list of items, or you can see if there is one that already exists. Common acronyms for musicians are, "Every Good Boy Does Fine," to remember the lines on the treble clef, and FACE to remember the spaces. Then you have "Good Boys Do Fine Always," for the lines on the bass clef, and "All Cows Eat Grass" for the spaces.

Another common acronym is HOMEs to remember the Great Lakes; Huron, Ontario, Michigan, Erie, and Superior.

Numbers

Have you ever felt the need to recite pi up to the 22,500 decimal digit? Maybe not, but have you ever really wanted to easily remember birthdays, PINs, passwords, phone numbers, and those types of things? Most everybody does. The problem is, our brains aren't always that great at memorizing numbers. The problem with numbers is that they are abstract concepts. While they may be represented visually by symbols, they don't feel all that real or fun for the brain. The brain tends to work better when it is provided with vibrant and lively images. Numbers don't come close in providing us that.

In our society, we are bombarded with new numbers: passcodes, PINs, ZIP codes, debit and credit card numbers, telephone numbers, and so on. Even if all of these numbers are programmed into your smartphone, it's still easier, not to mention, more secure to keep your most frequently used numbers in your mind.

When something doesn't mean something to you, it's quite hard to remember. Think about this for a minute. If you have ever owned a dog or even saw one at some point and I say the word dog, it is going to bring up all of the memories that you have about dogs and you are going to remember that word without difficulty. But when it comes to numbers, the majority of us don't have that kind of attachment to them.

So, if you are interested in remembering numbers, you have to give them meaning. Let's cover some of the best ways to memorize numbers in an easy manner.

- Create Associations

Everybody has a few numbers that are important to them, such as anniversaries, favorite football players, birthdays, or the amount of 10-cent wings you are able to devour at all-you-can-eat night. The secret to being able to remember new numbers is to figure out a connection between the numbers you need to remember and the numbers that you already have memorized.

If you are struggling to find an association for a number, try moving to the next number because this could end up triggering a memory that you will be able to use to link the first number. For example, if you need to memorize the number 1312, but you are struggling to associate 13 with something, you can move onto 12. 12 could make you think of *Cheaper by the Dozen,* and this could trigger the thought of a baker's dozen being 13.

- Make Long Numbers Short

The average person is only able to hold around seven arbitrary units of information at a time in their working memory. But when you chunk items in some fashion, you can improve your recall capacity. This is the main reason why phone numbers are separated into groups of digits instead of one long strand. Try to memorize this strand of numbers: 7986542872. If you try to interpret this as just a strand of 10 separate numbers, you will find this pretty hard to memorize. But if you are able to find two important dates within the sequence, you will only need to recall three chunks, and then remember won't be a problem.

- Try to Find Patterns

When it comes to long number strands, try to find relationships in the numbers. Do the first two numbers add up to equal the third? Do you notice a sequence of even or odd numbers? Then you can use those patterns to come up with a story with the more arbitrary numbers. For example, if you have the number 0123 7900, you can see the pattern of "0123" and then you can figure out how you can use this to remember 7900. For this example, you could come up with something like, once I max out my credit limit of $7900, I am going to have to start over at zero and build it up again a dollar at a time, 1, 2, 3.

- Actively Learn

Our muscles tend to remember things better than the brain, so you should just think the number. Say the number out loud at least three times. When you speak the number out loud, the brain will have to tell your mouth muscles how to say it and then your ears have to hear the words and pass along the information. This will make you have to use quite a few more areas of your brain. Then, you shouldn't stop there. You should then write the numbers down as well, or you could try to sing them to a memorable tune.

- Repeat

After you have memorized the number, set a time and do nothing but think about the number and any of the associations you have created with it. This should be done one hour after you have learned the number. Research has found that one hour after learning something new is the time in which the memory tends to be the most vulnerable to forgetting the information, degrading the information, or misinterpreting it. Then, in 24 hours, repeat the number again. Do this again one week after you have learned it, and then again after a month. The idea of all of this is to repeat the information around the time that you are about to forget the information, in increments of time that expand as time goes by, so that the number is stuck in your long-term memory. Whatever your brain has managed to learn after 30 days is probably going to stick with your.

- Visualize the Shape a Number Makes on a Keypad

There are a lot of people that will use this technique to remember phone numbers, but this is also great for ZIP codes, PINS, and credit card numbers, especially if you tend to learn better visually. This is extremely useful when numbers create an obvious pattern, such us an "L", "X", or a straight line.

- Convert to Images

There are two ways you could do this. You could set out to learn the major memory system, or you could simply assign the numbers 1 through 9 a letter equivalent, such as A equals 1, B equals 2, and so one. So if you have just created a new PIN number to 3647, you could change the numbers to the letters CFDG. You can then think up a sentence that uses those letters, like "Criminal Fiends Don't Get," and this could be fleshed out to, "criminal fiends don't get this number." This is likely something you would have an easier time remembering.

People who are memory competition competitors will take this method a step further and create an image or some action for every single number from 0 to 99. For instance, the number 36 would be a match and the number 47 would be a rock. They would then try to come up with a mental image that blends those two objects together. This is known as the major memory system, and can become quite confusing.

So, let's try to use the different pieces of information to remember a random ZIP code. Let's try 90089. Right off the bat you know that there are two zeros in the center, but that might not mean anything. There aren't any interesting patterns that they make on the keypad. Next we can chunk up the number: 90, 08, 89, 900. None of them stand out to me, so I'll do a quick Google search to see if anything comes up. The number 90 could refer to Nike Total 90, a sports apparel company that supplies soccer equipment. The number 89 could call up the 2017 film *89* that is about a soccer match between Liverpool and Arsenal in 1989. Then all you would need to remember is the extra 0 between the 90 and 89.

The next thing you would need to do is to repeat this after an hour, 24-hours, and then see how well you can remember it a week from when you learned, and so on. According to the experts, the odds are in your favor.

Places

Memorizing places are just as easy as memorizing numbers, maybe more so. The key memorizing everything is creating images that you can't forget. In ancient times, people would use mental images to help them memorize all types of material. These were commonly used for hundreds of years.

We're going to look at how to use a powerful technique to help you memorize the capitals of the US states. This technique can be used to remember any place that you want. This will work differently than our list of towns in Ireland. We aren't listing here. We are creating visualizations and associations.

This should be a fun technique so that you can recall the capitals, or whatever place you choose, with ease. You also want to make sure that you are clear with your images so that you don't end up confusing the city and states.

We know that the brain likes images, just think about how easy it is to picture your home. That means we need to create images just as vivid to help you associate the capital and state. These are going to be new images to you, so you will need to make them memorable. This means that you need to have a lot of fun when it comes to creating these mental images.

The secret to this technique uses actions, places, and objects that represent the sound of the names. This isn't all that tricky. As long as you get fairly close to it, your brain will step in and do the rest. The examples we will look at will show you how to do this. You will then be able to use this trick whenever you need for whatever you need.

1. Atlanta, Georgia

First, we are going to memorize the capital of Georgia, which is Atlanta. We are going to create a mental image so strong that we couldn't possibly think about a different or state. First, let's create a mental image for Atlanta. If you say this slowly, you get the sounds, at-lan-ta. To create a memorable image, maybe it becomes "ant land on." You only need to close to the real thing. A picture for "ant land on" we could picture an ant wearing a parachute having just jumped out of a plane.

Next, we have to think about Georgia. To me, I think of the name George. This could go one of two ways, Curious George or George

Washington. For our imagery, we'll go with George Washington. It's very easy to picture George's face on a dollar bill.

Now, we need to link the two images together. We want to make sure that we remember that Atlanta is the capital of Georgia. To do so, think about a one dollar bill with George Washington looking up into the sky with horror as an ant parachute down and lands on his face.

To lock this mental image into place, think about it a few times. It's an odd picture, so it should stick in your mind. We'll look at a couple of more examples to help you get the hang of this trick.

One note, however, is that when you are dealing with states like North and South Caroline or North and South Dakota, you want to make sure you differentiate the states so that you don't get confused. The easiest way to do this is to add a polar bear to the North state because polar bears live near the North Pole. Then add a penguin to the South state because penguins live near the South Pole.

2. Little Rock, Arkansas

The next state and capital we will look at is Little Rock, Arkansas. It's easy to picture a bunch of little rocks raining down from the sky to remember Little Rock. Then we need to break down Arkansas, which is pronounced ark-an-saw. This makes me think of an ark and a saw.

To create a link between the two, picture an ark sailing down the river. It is raining, but instead of raindrops, it's raining little rocks. These rocks hurt, so the sailor is trying to bat them away with a saw.

3. Frankfort, Kentucky

For our last example, we will create a mental image of Frankfort, Kentucky. To me, I would break Frankfort down into the sounds frank fork. For frank, we'll use a hot dog, and for fork, we will think of the metal eating utensil.

The word Kentucky breaks down into the sounds king tuck e. We will get rid of the e and just use king tuck. To bring together the images, we can picture a king holding a giant fork that he uses to tuck hot dogs (franks) down his pantaloons.

As long as you make sure that you practice recalling these images a few times after you come up with them, you shouldn't have a problem remembering them. Now, we could continue and go through every state, but these mental images work best when you come up with them yourself. They become personal to you at that point, and you will be less likely to forget them.

Names

The last thing we are going to look at is how to memorize names. This is something everybody probably wants to know how to do. There's nothing worse than running into a person that you know, but you can't think of their name. According to Psychology Today, this only gets worse with age. Nearly 85% of middle-aged and older adults will forget names.

It's understandable, though. When you meet a person, there is a lot that happens, from the way they look to the conversation and other distractions that take place. Rest assured, we can fix this problem so that you are no longer faced with that awkward moment. The technique we are going to look at is SISA: speak, imagination, specify, another.

1. Speak

First, you speak. This means that you repeat their name. When a person tells you their name, don't just smile and nod and then continue talking. You want to plug the name into your conversation. This can be done like so, "I'm Joseph." "Hi, Joseph, nice to meet you." If that doesn't work for you, can also ask a question using their name, such as "How long have you been working in marketing, Joseph?"

You can use their name throughout the conversation but do so sparingly. There's no need to come off overly salesy or repetitive. When you end the conversation, make sure you use their name again while looking them in the eye. Use this moment to commit it to memory.

2. Imagination

Several experts suggest that you create a mental image when you first hear a person's name. You can also create a verbal game by creating an alliterative sentence about the information you know about the person. For example, if you know they are from Maine and their name is Mary, it could be "Mary from Maine." The same can be done with their job.

To really engage your mind and memory, create a mental image of something that sounds like their name. This can then be combined with something that you know about them. If you met a person named Brock, it sounds like rock. If you knew he lived near their Rocky Mountains, then you could picture him hiking up a large rock.

3. Specify

The next thing to do is look at special features they have. When you notice these things about them, you can use them in your imagery from the last step so that you are certain about the person when you see them. This could even be a scent. Maybe they always wear the same perfume. The first thing that jumps out at you about them is the best feature that you should use in your mental image to help you remember their name.

Maybe they wear the same purple scarf no matter where they go. They could have really bright blue eyes that you can't help but notice. It could be that they have multicolored hair. Anything that you can pick out about that person that you couldn't possibly confuse with another person is exactly what you should add to your image.

4. Another

The last step to remembering a name is to associate their name with another person you already know. Chances are, you will immediately think of the other person you know when the new person introduces their self. This doesn't even have to be a person that you know personally.

Let's say you meet a woman named Carrie. This person is easy for you to associate with because your sister's name is Carrie. Then you meet a person named Charlie. You don't know any Charlie's personally, but you can associate them with the actor Charlie Sheen. The next time you meet either of these people, you will be able to remember their name by picturing the person you already know with them.

While this last tip I'm going to share isn't a part of the SISA technique, it can be helpful for a lot of people. Ask them to spell their name. This is mainly for people who have unusual names. This will help you to create a visual image of their name as they spell it out. If you are in a professional setting, you could ask for their business card instead.

Mind Mapping

Mind mapping was created by Tony Buzan. Mind mapping is a great way to get information into and out of your brain. It is a logical and creative means of taking notes and making notes that will map out ideas.

Every mind map will have certain things in common. They have an organizational structure that goes out from the center and uses images, color, words, symbols, and lines according to brain-friendly, simple concepts. This allows you to convert a monotonously long list into a highly organized, memorable, and colorful diagram that works with your brain's natural ability to do things.

A simple way to understand mind mapping is to compare it to a city map. The center of the city is where the main ideas are located. Main roads lead from this center to show your main thoughts. The secondary roads show your secondary thoughts, etc. Special shapes or images can stand for relevant ideas or interesting information.

The best thing about mind mapping is you can write down your ideas in any order when they enter your mind. You are not constrained by any specific order. Just write down any or all ideas and worry about organizing them later.

This wonderful technique has been used by more than 250 million people throughout the world to help with tasks like communicating information, studying, teaching, managing projects, organizing, finding new opportunities, brainstorming, and a lot more.

Mind maps can be used for all cognitive functions like analysis, creativity, learning, and memory. This process involves a combination of visual-spatial arrangement, color, and imagery. It maps out your thoughts by using keywords that make associations in the brain that sparks more ideas.

There are several software programs out there that will help you organize your thoughts, and it will export them into an easy to read list.

It is possible to mind map with paper and pen but why not use technology and save yourself time. There are many elements to think about like the center image, keywords, colors, images, and branches.

A mind map is an external mirror of your own natural thinking that makes it easier by using powerful graphics. This gives us a key to unlock the unlimited potential of our brains.

There are five main characteristics to mind mapping:

- The main focus, subject, or idea is the central image

- The main themes run from the center image like branches

- These branches will have a main image or word drawn on its lines

- Lesser important topics are on the "twigs" of the branches

- These branches create a connected structure

How to Mind Map

Here are the steps to create a mind map:

1. Figure out a central idea

This is the starting point of your mind map and will represent the main topic you want to explore.

This needs to be in the center of the paper and need to include an image that shows your main topic. This will draw attention to and will trigger further association because our brains will respond better to visual stimulation.

Take time to make the main idea personal. This strengthens the connection you have with the content of the mind map.

2. Add branches

Now you need to get your creative juices going and add in some branches. The main branch that goes from the center image is the main ideas. You can explore each branch in great detail by adding smaller branches.

The best thing about a mind map is that you can constantly add new branches and you aren't restricted to only a few options. The structure will come naturally as you add in more ideas while your brain draws associations from the various concepts.

3. Add keywords

Once you have added a branch to your mind map, you need to add key ideas. One important aspect to mind mapping is putting one word on every branch. Using just one word will spark numerous associations as compared to using a lot of words or phrases.

Let's say you want to throw a surprise party for your boss. You create a branch that says "surprise party." Now you have limited the brainstorm to just aspects of a party. If you only use the word "surprise," you can go out with other words like cake, presents, party, decorations, etc.

Having just one word on each branch works great for chunking information into themes. Using keywords triggers connections if the brain and lets you remember more information.

4. Color the branches

Mind mapping encourages the entire brain to think because it sparks numerous cortical skills like special, creative, numerical, and logical.

Overlapping these skills will make your brain synergetic and keeps it working at its optimal level. When you keep these skill isolated from each other doesn't help the brain develop. This is what the brain was designed to do.

An example of the entire brain thinking is to color code our mind map. Color coding will link the visual and the logical. This allows your brain to make shortcuts. This, in turn, lets you analyze, highlight, identify, and categorize more connections that you might not have thought about before.

Colors make things more engaging and appealing as compared to monochromatic, plain images.

5. Use images

Images can convey more information than an essay, sentence, or a word. They get instantly processed by the brain and act as stimuli to help you recall information. Images are a universal language that can overcome language barriers.

We have been taught from a young age to process images. Before children learn to read in any language, they can see pictures in their minds that get linked to concepts. This is the main reason behind mind mapping.

Increase Reading Speed

Do you want to be able to read a book effortlessly and quickly? Do you want to learn how to speed read without forgetting what you have just read?

Many people think that speed reading is hard to learn, but it is an art that can be learned by using the right tools and exercises. They think you have to learn how to speed read at an early age and it can't be learned when you get older. This isn't true, as many people have learned to speed read at an older age.

It doesn't matter if you are skimming through blog posts, looking through files for work, or browsing a book, you probably do some sort of reading each day. Trying to get through dense textbooks is hard on your eyes, mentally exhausting, and time-consuming.

With some practice, you will be able to read through dozens of pages in just a few minutes.

1. Scan or skim

Scanning or skimming are two techniques that involve looking for the most important parts first. This will get you ready for what is to come. You probably know a little bit about the text, to begin with, so you won't be surprised if you come upon a confusing part.

Remember that while you are scanning or skimming, it works best when you are reading non-fiction books. It can be done with novels, just skim the chapter to find major plot points, key dialogue points, and character development. Next read at a faster pace than normal.

2. Don't subvocalize

This is the most common factor that slows down reading. This is the most critical and hardest habit to break when learning how to speed read. Sometimes we are limited by how long it takes us to pronounce every word on the page. This is the way the majority reads. We "speak" every word in our mind. This will slow down your reading to how fast you speak. This is around 300 words per minute.

When we say a word out loud, it takes a specific amount of time to pronounce the word. Truth is, we don't have to pronounce the words when we read. We can just absorb them.

If you have ever been reading and realized your lips were moving while you read, this is still subvocalization.

This habit is so embedded in our brains that breaking free of this sound completely impossible. A great trick is to choose a word and look at it for a few minutes in complete silence. There is going to be some subvocalization but just look at the words without wanting to pronounce it. A new habit will be for form.

A good tip to defeat this habit is to begin looking at and thinking about words without needing to pronounce them. This part might feel completely weird at first, and that is normal. You just need to worry about looking at the words without wanting to hear how they sound.

With some practice, you will begin to see a difference between speaking the word and just letting it enter your mind. When you can do this, you will have torn down the largest barrier between speed reading and yourself.

Our brains and eyes can process words a lot faster than that. If you can stop the voice in your head, you could double your reading speed.

If you subvocalize, it is hard to learn how to read faster. This is a hard habit to break. The best and easiest way is to become mindful of it to keep yourself distracted. You could use your finger, chew gum, or listen to music.

3. Read phrases instead of words

In order to increase your reading speed, be mindful of what your eyes are doing. Many people can scan about one and a half inch chunk of words. This depends on the type of text and font size which is usually made up of about five words. Instead of reading every single word, move your eyes and jump from chunk to chunk. Use your peripheral vision to speed up at the start and end of every line. Focus on blocks instead of the first and last words.

If you look at every fifth word, this allows you to take in more at a time and will help you stop vocalizing. Just like all things, it is going to take time and training to be able to do this well. Beginning with textbooks would be the best place to start.

Using a pen or your finger to point at every chunk of words helps you learn the right way to move your eyes over the text. It encourages you to stop subvocalizing.

4. Stop re-reading

The largest time sucker for many people is going back and reading paragraphs or sentences that they didn't understand the first time. They think if they didn't completely understand each word the whole book won't make sense.

You will eventually realize that you aren't getting any comprehension when you re-read. The confusing parts will make sense in context, or they aren't needed to be able to enjoy the book.

An untrained person will use back-skipping or subconscious rereading by misplaced fixation and regression or conscious rereading that makes up about 30 percent of their total reading time. That is a lot of time. Stop having to completely comprehend each thing that is going on or being said. You will quit wasting time reading things you have already read.

5. Read more

Reading is just like all worthy pursuits; it is a skill that will take time to develop. The more you practice, the better you get. Many people think that setting goals are silly. Reading isn't a race. Setting goals will force you to create more time to read. The more you read, the faster you will get.

Remember the best way to enjoy books is to read them at your own pace. Books are meant to be savored. Who cares if you spend countless hours enjoying a great story? There will always be books in the world, and only so much time. I would be better to enjoy the books you want to than to breeze through ones you don't care about.

6. Preview the text

Looking at a film's trailer before you watch the movie will give you some context and allows you to know what you should expect. The same holds true for previewing text before reading it. It will prepare you to get an understanding of what you will be reading. In order to preview text, scan it from start to finish. Pay attention to bullet points, large or bold font, subheadings, and headings. To understand it better, skim through the introductory paragraphs and conclusions. Try to find transitions sentences and look at graphs or images. See how the author structured the text.

7. Have an attack plan

Approaching the text strategically will make a difference in how effectively you will understand the material. The first thing to do is think about what your goals are. What is it you want to learn from this material? Write down some questions you would like to have answered at the end. Figure out what the author's goals were when they wrote the material. Their goal might be describing the whole history of Ancient Greece. Your goal might be just to answer a question about a woman's role in politics. If your goal is more inclusive than the author's, try to find and only read the sections you need.

Change up your attack plan by the kind of material you are reading. If you need to read a science textbook or a large legal file, you will need to read specific passages slower and more carefully than you would read a magazine.

8. Be mindful

In order to read fast and be able to comprehend what you have read takes concentration and focus. Get rid of interruptions, distractions, and external noises. If you realize you are thinking about what you are going to eat instead of focusing on what you are reading, bring your mind back to the material gently. Most readers will read some sentences without actually focusing, then they waste time reading it again to make sure they understand it. If you attentively and carefully approach your reading, you will realize if you don't understand something and this will save you time.

9. Don't read each section

It is a total myth that you have to read each section of text. If you aren't reading something that is important, skip sections that aren't relevant to your purpose. Selective reading makes it possible for you to find the main ideas in most texts.

10. Do a summary

You aren't finished when you have read the last word in a book. Once you have finished reading, write some sentences to summarize what you have just read. Answer the questions you wrote before you began reading. Did you find everything you wanted to find? When you take some time after you have finished reading to write down what you learned, to think, and to gather the information, you will make the material more solid in your mind so you can have better recall. If you are a verbal or visual learner, create a mind map to tell another person what you have learned.

11. Do some timed runs

You have to strategically approach the text, read it actively, and summarize it. All of this takes practice. If you would love to improve your reading speed, time to see how many pages or words you can read per minute. Once you are able to read faster, check in to see if you are happy with how well you are comprehending things.

12. Figure out your baseline

In order to get faster as speed reading, you have to be able to recognize your growth. Before you can measure this, you have to have a baseline. Once you have your baseline, you have to measure your reading periodically and compare it to this baseline.

A good resource to track your results is ReadingSoft.com. This provides you with a consistent, rapid measurement of how fast you are reading. When you take tests regularly, it will be easier to recognize your growth, and this will give you all the motivation you will need to continue.

The main problem with understanding your baseline is it is hard to translate into normal terms when talking about reading a specific amount of words per minute. It is a practical place to start, but it is more important to know how long it takes you to read a page.

If a normal person takes five to ten minutes to read a page, speed readers only need more than two to three minutes. This means that a 200-page book could be read in 400 minutes by a speed reader where a normal reader will take between 1000 to 2000 minutes.

This means a normal reader will spend an extra 13 or so hours on the book. That is more than one half of a day that has been lost.

It isn't easy jumping from reading for 17 hours to being a speed reader. There will be some obstacles in your way, but many of them can be dealt with easily.

13. Use pointers

Using your finger as a guide while reading is usually reserved for children, most people stop doing it once they have learned to read. This trick is handy when learning to speed read.

The largest hurdle in learning to speed read isn't learning the skill but in getting rid of old habits that stop us. One of these habits is reading without a guide. When learning to speed read, a guide is a necessity. This one isn't negotiable.

When you use a guide, your main goal is moving the guide at a constant pace. You should never stop or slow down your finger. It needs to slide from side to side at a uniform speed. By doing this, you will notice if you get stuck or lose any momentum. This is easier than trying to follow along and moving your eyes as quickly as possible.

When you try to move your eyes quickly, you will not be able to maintain a fluid motion because you will eventually hit an obstacle. This will cause you to backtrack, and this causes confusion.

If you have to do this twice on one page, this will add 30 seconds per page. That adds up to an hour and a half that is lost to backtracking on the whole book. You have to learn to think about speed reading as a marathon instead of a race.

Pointers aren't limited to just your finger. You could use a pen, marker, ruler, whatever is handy for you.

14. Don't read unimportant, small words

To understand the way speed readers get fast is to understand that not all words are created equal. There are a lot of small words that don't help you but try to force you to read them. This will only hurt you in the long run.

If you look back at the above point that adding an extra 30 seconds per page could translate to a whole hour and a half think about what could be done when you get rid of all the "to," "is," "the," "if," and other small words. This concept will save you time, but it is yet another skill you need to develop.

The best part of skipping small words is they don't contribute any useful information. This means that skipping them won't ruin your reading experience. Cool, right?

When you skip words, you will get more done. To train yourself to skip the small words, it is simply realizing that you don't need to pay any attention to them. Just let your eyes move across them.

With time, your brain will learn to skip them, and you will be able to scan sentences while skipping insignificant words.

Alternatives to Speed Reading

Reading might not be something you enjoy doing, but you do enjoy books. What do you do now? There are alternatives to you actually reading books.

Many books available to the public can also be found as an audiobook. This allows you to "read" a book while walking, jogging, working, doing laundry, or whatever needs to be done during your day. Some platforms even give you a free trial period to start.

You might have been in a bookstore and found a book that looked very interesting, but the book was just too thick to even think about reading, so you put it back. Days later you are still wondering about that book. What do you do?

There is an app for that. It is called Blinkist. The Blinkist team reads books, finds the main points, and explains them in an easy 15-minute summary. It is basically a web version to the small paperback CliffNotes that most high school students would use to help them on book reports.

Maintaining Memory

You might have taken a class on something to help you in your job. Maybe it was a book about your field of expertise. You might have taken the latest computer course and learned how to use a new system. Within a few weeks or months, you have forgotten everything.

If we don't apply the new knowledge, it is very easy to forget what you learned. Maybe you take notes like crazy while in class. Do you ever get those notes out after the course is over to read back over what you learned? If not, this is the main reason we forget what we have learned.

Everything in this book will help you with your memory so it is extremely important to read this book many times so you get everything you can out of it.

Review

Let's look at how beneficial it is to review information while we explore strategies that will also help.

When learning new information, it is remembered best right after we learn it. We will forget the details as time goes by. Within just a few days, we are only able to recall just a bit of what we had learned.

In order to remember things for a long time, we have to move the information out of our short-term memory into our long-term memory. Short-term memory is the things we currently think about.

To help us do this, we have to review everything we learn and do it often. It will take time to move this information into long-term memory but reviewing it over and over again will help us do it.

These strategies can be used in everyday business situations while helping you improve your memory - things like your client list, details about your client, or recalling information for a presentation.

Reviewing Effectively

Let's look at some strategies that are useful to help you remember information in the long run.

1. Immediately review

Take a few minutes and look over the material right after you learned it. This will help you know that you understand the material. It will reduce the time you need to relearn parts of it when you need it in the future.

While you are reading over the material again, use effective strategies to be sure you are reading intelligently and efficiently. For example, if you have finished reading a chapter in a book, you might only need to look at certain headings and the chapter conclusion to begin putting information into your long-term memory.

2. Rewrite things

Reorganizing and rewriting your notes is a great way to look over information.

This may sound like a waste of time, but rewriting can be an efficient method to reinforce what you are learning. Research has shown that rewriting notes will help clarify what we understand.

An easy way to do this is to put the information we learn into mind maps. These are great for rewriting notes since they force us to make connections between themes and concepts.

You could write down the main points into bullet style or just tidy up your original notes.

3. Schedule time to review

It takes a repeat effort to move information into long-term memory. This is why you need to review information many times.

It is best to do a review one day after the class, then again in a week, a month, and then review the notes a few months from here on out.

Be sure you schedule the time for reviews, or they will get pushed to the side when an urgent matter comes up. Put these reviews on a to-do list or daily planner.

You will find it useful to rewrite your notes during these reviews. Try to jot down what you remember about the class, and compare this to the original notes. This will pinpoint any information that you might have forgotten plus it will refresh your memory.

Getting enough sleep will help your memory, too. Research has shown that we can remember more if we get plenty of sleep. Read on to learn more.

Naps

Researchers have known for a long time that sleep helps memory. Poor sleep has been linked to problems with memory. Researchers have also found that sleeping right after you have learned new things could improve memory retention. If you want a quick memory boost, you should try taking a power nap.

Power Naps Improve Retention

Researchers at Saarland University looked at how an hour long nap helped memory recall in 41 volunteers. These people were asked to learn individual words along with pairs of words. At the end of this learning time, the volunteers were given a test to see what they remembered. The next part of the experiment asked half of the volunteers to watch a movie while the others were allowed to take a nap.

The volunteers were given another test to see how many individual words and pairs of words they remembered. The volunteers who were allowed to take a power nap remembered more words than the ones who watched a movie.

A nap that is between 45 minutes to one hour will improve how well a person can retrieve memory.

Researchers noted the volunteers who took the power nap didn't do any better on the test after the nap. They scored the same on both tests. The volunteers who watched the movie scored a lot worse after watching the movie. Researchers stated that memory after a nap is almost the same as memory after learning a new skill. Power naps should be confused with "microsleep" which could be dangerous.

Look Inside Our Brain

The researchers didn't just look at how well people performed on tests. They wanted to figure out what was happening inside the brain especially what the hippocampus was doing. The hippocampus plays a crucial role in consolidating and transferring the information into long-term memory. Researchers used EEGs to look at "sleep spindles." They thought that if something was strong in memory, the more "sleep spindles" will show up on an EEG.

To minimize the probability that words could be recalled from the prior association, researchers gave the volunteers 90 individual words with 120 meaningless pairs of words. Instead of pairing up the words that that would have any logical association like "peanut – butter" or "table – lamp," they used combinations that didn't have any relation to one another like "juice – carpet."

Using familiarity isn't useful here when trying to remember word pairs since they hadn't ever heard these combinations of words before. They had to access specific memories from their hippocampus.

What exactly does this mean for anybody who would like to improve their memory? Short naps in school or at the office might be enough to improve their learning. When people are in an environment to learn, they need to think a lot about the wonderful effects of sleep.

When you have an important exam looming ahead, think about taking a quick nap right before the test.

Meditation

Having problems with memory happens to everyone as we get older. No one is immune to this problem. There is good news. Meditation has been proven to be a natural solution to help bother short- and long-term memory. Here are some reasons why:

1. Mind strength training

When we begin to age, our mental capacity will peak and then start to decline. When you use your mind to reach higher levels of focus and concentration is essential to meditation. If you can learn to do this, you will be exercising and strengthening your mind. This will help keep it in great shape. When meditating, we are working our mental muscles and thus prolonging our brain's life. This will keep us from suffering from memory loss.

2. Meditation can slow down the process of aging

Stress is a huge factor in the characteristics of aging like memory loss. It can be reduced significantly after starting a meditation program. Most scientists and doctors think that meditation to be the "fountain of youth" for our brains and bodies.

3. Meditation taps into our memory stores

Meditation could help you remember things that you might have forgotten years ago. Since the brain doesn't discard memories, these memories remain stored in our brains subconsciously. We just need to access them.

The tools we need to access our memories are the thing that we lose. Meditation is the best way to harness the subconscious mind. This lets us retrieve information that we thought was completely gone. Meditation allows this to happen naturally and normally.

4. Meditation will stimulate regions of the brain associated with memory

While you meditate, the frontal lobe and hippocampus which are the storage centers for short- and long-term memories, will light up.

This means you are flexing your memory muscle while you are meditation. You information storage centers will multiply and makes sure your brain keeps the ability to store new memories.

5. Meditation will increase focus

We are going to have memory problems from time to time. This comes from not paying attention to specific subjects like names of people you meet. When we can use mindfulness and learn to live in the moment, we will have more recall. Meditation teaches us to do this. We will be able to remember more details since we have actively stored them away as memories and give them significance.

If you would like to give your memory a boost, meditation is the best, most tested, product out there. The benefits of meditation go way beyond our brains.

Turning Procrastination into Productivity

People who like procrastinating will put things off for days even if they know it should have been done two days ago.

What Procrastination Looks Like

Everyone puts off working on things we don't like to do every now and then. Nobody likes making phone calls that are just going to stress us out. Who has ever heard of someone who likes washing the windows, taking out the garbage, or washing the car? Most people will do these things occasionally. People who procrastinate will do this all the time. This is when the problems begin.

Stress Factor

Procrastination can lead to stress. Procrastination makes wishes and plans fail when we should be feeling fulfillment. Vacation packages and theatre tickets sell out before procrastinators can reserve them. Jobs get taken by other people, deadlines go past, and planes leave without them.

Negative Effects

A Procrastination Research Group in Canada at Carleton University created an online survey. They asked a question: "To what extent is procrastination having a negative impact on your happiness?" They received 2700 responses. Around 56 percent replied with "very much" or "quite a bit." About 18 percent replied with "extreme negative effect."

Threatens Happiness

Most of the time procrastination gets trivialized. People who procrastinate will suffer if they fail to reach their goals or their careers crash. In the long run, procrastination can become more than a threat to productivity, happiness, and health: it could carry this threat into our surroundings like community and companies.

Traits

How can you recognize a procrastinator? They will avoid telling the truth about their abilities. They might prefer to have service jobs. They will focus on the past and don't act on intentions. They will make poor estimates on their time. These characteristics are linked to anxiety, depression, self-confidence, self-control, self-deception, non-competitiveness, perfectionism, and low self-esteem.

No Easy Answers

There aren't any easy answers. It isn't about managing time. When you tell a person who procrastinates to "just do it" is similar to telling someone who is depressed to "just cheer up." We have to look at the way people procrastinate to know why they do it and figure out how to fix it.

Why We Procrastinate?

There are many reasons why people procrastinate. Some people who procrastinate usually had authoritarian fathers. People who procrastinate use it as a way to rebel their demands.

Other people put the blame on parents who didn't allow their children room to create their imagination.

Other people think that procrastinators act and think along the lines of "wishes and dreams" while other people get on with their obligations. People who procrastinate will have disorganized thoughts. This means they will be forgetful and don't plan things very well.

How We Procrastinate

Research in the field of procrastination is relatively new, but scientists are beginning to describe different ways to procrastinate. Two common types are decisional and behavioral procrastination.

Decisional Procrastination

This strategy puts off making decisions if you are dealing with choices or conflicts. People that practice high levels of decisional procrastination are afraid of making mistakes and are usually perfectionists. These people seek more information about things before trying to make decisions if they are even able to make a decision at all.

If a procrastinator is over informed, they are in danger of falling prey to self-sabotage called optional paralysis. They make countless choices and feel unable to pick the right one because they are afraid of picking an option that isn't perfect.

Behavioral Procrastination

This is a self-sabotage strategy that lets people shift blame to avoid action. A student might make a bad grade on a test and use an excuse of procrastination. They would rather create an illusion of lack of effort instead of ability. They will then blame any failure on not having enough time.

Procrastinators usually have self-doubt and low self-esteem. They also worry about how people judge how they do things. People who procrastinate look at their self-worth by looking at their abilities. According to this logic, if you don't finish a task, your ability can't ever be judged.

Failure to adequately perform and prolonged procrastination makes a cycle of behavior that will defeat one's self. This will result in a downward spiral of their self-esteem. Self-inflicted shame and degradation like this will translate into mental health problems and stress at some time.

Steps for Change

The very first step to change is insight. The second step is understanding. Once that has been taken care of, then taking a course on behavior modification therapy might help if your procrastination is causing problems in your relationship or work. There isn't a bandage solution for procrastination, anything that will help you take firm steps will help to rebuild healthy levels of self-esteem and achievement along with helping you feel good about yourself.

Purpose

Why in the world do we treat ourselves this way? The solution seems very simple: "just do it". The reality is a lot more complicated, and what makes it worse is procrastination is written in our DNA. Procrastination runs in the family. It is linked with impulsivity and creates a catch-all that regulates our behaviors. Above all that, research says that procrastination is a trait that will be with you for life.

So, what about people who procrastinate? Are they all doomed to a life of absently watching music videos on YouTube?

Great news, no we aren't doomed. Just like people who are inhibited, they can learn to loosen up. People who are worriers can learn to let it go. People who procrastinate can find ways to help them resist impulses and focus.

There are many faces of procrastination. It might simply be choosing pleasure over a discipline. It might be hard to avoid things that are negative. Sometimes we get paralyzed by expectations that become overwhelming. Not to worry, here are some reasons why we procrastinate and a way to overcome each one:

1. Not an urgent task

It might be a deadline for the end of the week, a ringing phone, a crying baby, whatever it is we will pay attention to the thing that is in front of you.

It is hard to prioritize things when they aren't urgent. From saving for retirement to getting the basement organized, everyone has things that they will never do. Because of this, small and large tasks will sit on the bottom of the to-do list for months and maybe years being neglected.

- Solution: Look at the bigger picture

This tendency is annoying but has some significance in evolution. People have been wired to think about present needs stronger than what we might need in the future. This phenomenon is called temporal discounting. On our face is the present, and we pay it more attention.

This remedy takes a broader perspective instead of being nit-picky about the details. Look at daily tasks as if looking at a bigger picture.

If you want to go back to school, but just can't find the time to do it, you take a few steps back. Would this change your life? What are your goals about education? What is your big picture? Looking at a new perspective can help you take action.

When you have decided it is time to take action, now you are faced with a new type of procrastination:

2. Not knowing how to begin or what might come next

We often find ourselves procrastinating because we don't know what to do. We feel disorganized, confused, or overwhelmed. We won't begin since we don't understand what the first step should be.

This type of procrastination isn't just avoiding the task. It is avoiding a negative emotion. Nobody likes to feel clueless or incompetent; this is why we turn to Netflix instead of cleaning the bathroom. We put off what we should do now by doing other things that are more interested. This is called productive procrastination. Anybody who has tried to organize their desk or does shopping online instead of doing their reports will understand this. When we find that perfect outfit before our date makes us feel like we are ready to go.

• Solution: Create confusion

The main point is knowing it is completely normal to feel stupid when beginning a task that you haven't done before.

Create some confusion into the task at hand. Turn the first step into "figuring out the steps". If screaming into a pillow will get you started, them make that step number one.

Others might need another person to help them think. Brainstorm with a friend or coworker to figure out where you should begin.

It is perfectly normal for the start of the task to include messes, do-overs, and turnarounds. It will only feel bad if you make it feel bad.

3. Afraid of failing

Having a bit of perfectionism is bad. Having high standards will lead to high-quality work. Beyonce, Serena Williams, and Bruno Mars all claim to be perfectionists. At time having high standards will backfire. We will blow off projects because we have convinced ourselves that there is no way we can make the standards we have set.

- Solution: Untangle self-worth and performance

Procrastination and perfectionism are linked together. It isn't the high standards that hold you back but the high standards that get mixed with you believing you performance is connected to your self-worth. This combination can stop you in your tracks.

Remember the critical difference between you and the things you achieve. There is a lot more to you than what you accomplish. Just think about your knowledge, taste, politics, friends, travels, experiences, passions, family, identity, the way you treat others, and the challenges you have overcome.

4. We work better under pressure

Most of us know or might have been that child in high school or college who opens up their textbook just before a final exam and still manage to do better than others who have studied all semester.

- Solution: know yourself

Those children were planning ahead in their own way. There are two kinds of procrastination: active and passive. Active procrastination contains strategy. For people who work well under pressure and like the adrenaline rush and focus that comes with having deadlines and they choose to start very close to that deadline.

Passive procrastination is what most people think about when they hear the word procrastination. They get distracted by videos of bicycle riding dogs or squirrels surfing.

It seems like the choice will pay off, too. Passive procrastination can negatively affect a person's GPA, but an active procrastinator's grades will be just fine. We need to know ourselves. If you are a night owl and thrive in that environment, put on a pot of coffee and open that book at midnight.

5. We don't want to do it

What we should do is boring, hard, it's almost quitting time, it's Friday, and we don't want to be here.

There are things that nobody wants to do like getting out of the recliner and going to bed, calling tech support, and taxes. What are you going to do?

- Solution: Compensate and measure

Many college students who loved to procrastinate did it just because there were other more fun alternatives. To their own selves, they aren't blowing off work; they had all intentions of studying but just not now.

These procrastinators know themselves as well as active procrastinators do. They compensated their procrastination by intending to study earlier and more than other non-procrastinators. Basically, they set time aside from the beginning. Guess what? They studied more than the non-procrastinators not a lot but more.

If you would like to stop procrastinating, see the big picture. Understand it is fine to be confused and dazed at the start. Remember you are worthy and always go beyond your achievements. You have to know yourself. Work with your procrastination just as it is and not how you want it to be.

Goals

Many say that humans are geared toward setting and achieving goals. Goals are a part of everyone's life. What you do in your spare time, the things you want to achieve at work, how you behave in your relationships. All things come down to priorities and the things you want to accomplish in all aspects. It doesn't matter if it is a conscious or subconscious choice.

If you don't set objectives or goals, life will become chaotic happening that is out of your control. You are just coincidence's plaything. Accomplishments such as putting a person on the moon, inventing the computer, etc. are the results of goals that were set at some point in time. It was somebody's vision that was recorded and realized.

Why Set SMART Goals?

Setting SMART goals will bring you structure and makes it easier to track your goals. You won't have vague resolutions; SMART goals will create verifiable goals that take you toward your objective along with clear milestones and an estimate of how attainable the goal is. Each objective can be turned into a SMART goal and can bring you closer to your reality.

Setting SMART goals is the best effective but least used tools to achieve goals. When you have created the outline for your goals, it is time to set intermediary goals. By using a SMART checklist, you will be able to evaluate your objectives. Setting SMART goals will create transparency. It will clarify the way the goal came into existence.

What Does SMART Mean?

Try to think of a goal you would like to set right now whether it be professional or personal. In order for your goal to be a SMART one, it needs the following criteria:

Specific

What is it you want to achieve? If you can be very specific in your description, you will have a better chance of getting it. Setting a SMART goal will clarify the difference in saying "I want to have a lot of money" and saying "I want to make $50,000 each month for ten years by creating the next video game craze."

Questions you should ask while setting your goals:

- Exactly what is it I would like to achieve?

- When?

- With whom?

- Where?

- Are there any limitations or conditions?

- How?

- Why do I want this goal?

- Are there any alternatives in attaining this goal?

Measurable

A measurable goal means you have identified exactly what you want to feel, hear, and see when you have reached your goal. This means breaking down the goal into elements that can be measured. You have to have concrete evidence. Being happy isn't evidence. Quitting smoking because you want a healthier lifestyle is.

Goals that are measurable will go a long way to define exactly what you want. Being able to define the physical manifestations of the goal will make it clearer and therefore easier to reach.

Attainable

Can you attain your goal? This means you need to investigate to see if the goal is totally acceptable to you. You need to weigh the costs, time, and effort against the profits or other obligation you have in your life.

If you don't have the talent, money, or time to reach your goal, you will be miserable and fail. This isn't saying that you can't make something that seems to be impossible and make it possible but planning and doing it.

There isn't anything wrong with shooting for the stars.

Relevant

Is the goal relevant to you? Do you really want to run your own company, be the next breakout artist, have a husband and family? You have to decide if you have the guts to do it.

If you don't have specific skills, you can take classes. If you don't have specific resources, you can find them on the internet.

The big questions are: "Why do I want to reach this goal?" "What is my objective behind this goal?" "Will this goal actually achieve that?"

You could have a larger team to make you perform better, but will it actually?

Timely

We've all heard the old expression: "Time is money." Make a plan of everything you do. Everyone knows a deadline will cause people to jump into action. Make deadlines for yourself and go after them. Keep them flexible and realistic. This will keep your morale high. If you are too rigid on time, it could harm the outcome instead of helping you achieve your goals. This isn't how you want to achieve your goals.

One other thing that is important when creating SMART goals is creating it positively. Remember when you focus on something it will increase. If you focus on NOT doing something, you will only think about that one thing. And it increases. Try to achieve daily discipline.

Time Limits

Never think about breaks as a specific number during the day like five or 12. The main question is how long you should work before you take a break.

75 to 90 Minutes

It has been suggested that you take a break after working for 75 to 90 minutes. This is the amount of time where you will be able to concentrate and get work done. This is the length of time most college classes are held. Most professional musicians will practice for this time limit, too.

Working for 75 to 90 minutes will take advantage of our brain's modes: consolidation and focusing. If people work and then take a 15-minute break, it helps their brain consolidate and retain information better.

This works by breaking a pattern, which is called pulse and pause. It expends energy and then renews it. Research has shown that humans will move from full energy and complete focus to mental and physical fatigue every 90 minutes.

When we pay attention to our bodies, we would realize our bodies are sending signals for us to rest and renew. We override these signals with sugar, energy drinks, and coffee. Some might tap into their reserves until they are completely depleted.

52 Minutes

There might be times when you don't have to work for an hour and a half. The good news is you can work for shorter periods of time and still get the benefits of taking a break. Workers who are more productive take regular breaks. They work for 52 minutes and take 17-minute breaks. These employees achieved more tasks without having to work longer. Having regular breaks caused them to be more efficient.

The reason productive employees can get more done in shorter time periods is that they are well rested during working time. They work with purpose during their 52 minutes.

25 Minutes

The Pomodoro Technique is another option. It breaks up extended focus time into short work periods. This technique works for 25 minutes and then takes a break for five minutes. This technique was developed by Francesco Cirillo. He named it after the kitchen timer that was shaped like a tomato he used. This technique works best when one task needs your complete focus.

Finding the correct amount of time for your breaks will take some trial and error. The point isn't the length of the work or break time. It is finding out what cycle works for you. A person's cognitive capacity will decline during the day. You have to create mental breaks to recharge yourself and maintain productivity.

Using the Break

All breaks aren't created equal. People will pick a break time that doesn't always work for their benefit. The popular breaks such as venting about a problem, drinking a cup of coffee, or eating a snack can cause more fatigue.

Many people will choose these things as ways to cope with fatigue, but these breaks don't renew energy. In order to make a break work for you, you have to be able to mentally disengage from work. Morning breaks might include meditation, helping a friend, or talking to a coworker. Afternoon breaks are the most important and need specific activities. The body's energy will go down throughout the day and breaks could reenergize you.

Do some sort of exercise. Regular exercise can increase our energy level and improves metabolism. Most people think that including exercise into a work day is too much. This is why doing longer breaks is very effective. Simple exercises might include a bike ride in the park or walking for 20 minutes.

Naps are a popular afternoon break. Short naps can be invigorating. Many people worry they will fall asleep and sleep longer than they should. There is a very simple solution. It is a little thing called an alarm clock.

Taking a break might like you are slacking off, they are very important to your productivity. It isn't the time you spend working. It is what you get accomplished during that time. Get rid of time as a way to measure success. You can get more done when you take breaks to energize yourself.

Interesting Facts

Foods

If you are worried about memory loss, you could find help in your kitchen. Here is a list of foods that you could add to your diet that have been proven to help with mental clarity.

- Green tea: You might have heard about the antioxidant power of green tea. It can also help boost your memory, too.

- Blueberries: Berries have an antioxidant pigment called anthocyanin that can increase a person's ability to remember. One study that was done over a three-month period showed an improved recall in older adults that drank blueberry juice.

- Extra-virgin olive oil: This oil contains hydroxytyrosol that can increase messages going to the brain and helps with memory.

- Dark chocolate: Any dark chocolate that is at least 70 percent cocoa has flavanols that increase the blood flow to the brain.

- Almonds: These are excellent brain food since they contain proteins that can boost the production of the nerve chemical that can enhance memory

Coffee and Gum

If you have been looking for something to help your memory, look no further than your coffee cup. There is a theory that caffeine can help to improve your cognitive function. Coffee can also lower your risk of developing Alzheimer's disease if drunk during midlife.

If you aren't a coffee drinker, you can try the "pretend coffee" drinks such as chocolate cream, mocha, vanilla, and Swiss to help improve your memory. If you love your daily coffee, this is another reason to continue with your morning cup or two.

What Research is Saying

Recent studies have shown that coffee can improve memory. The study involved 160 volunteers. They were shown various pictures and objects and were told to identify them as either outdoor or indoor items.

After five minutes have passed, they were either given a placebo or a 200mg caffeine pill. They waited 24 hours and were shown the exact same pictures along with some different ones. They were asked to tell whether the pictures were "similar," "old," or "new."

Researchers noted that both groups could accurately tell if the pictures were new or old. The volunteers who were given the caffeine pill had a better memory than the ones who took the placebo. Giving the pill after showing the pictures demonstrated that caffeine improved the volunteer's memories instead of other probabilities like the improvement in focus or concentration.

They did other experiments with 300 and 100 mg doses of caffeine. The performance was better with the 200 mg doses when compared with the 100 mg dose. There wasn't any improvement with the 300 mg of caffeine when compared to the 200 mg doses.

What they concluded was that a dose of 200 mg of caffeine-enhanced memory better than any other does.

They also found that memory wasn't improved if the volunteers were given caffeine one hour before the identification test.

There are many ways that caffeine might help long-term memory. It might block a molecule called adenosine and keep it from stopping norepinephrine. This hormone can have good effects on memory. Further research is being done to understand the mechanisms of how caffeine affects memory.

When older adults drink coffee, they showed improved working memory when compared to others who don't drink coffee.

Another study found that bees who drank coffee remembered floral scents when compared to bees who drank sucrose. The main question with this study is if this can actually translate to humans.

When combining coffee with sugar, research showed that a person's concentration or attention, verbal memory, and reaction time all improved when compared to others who only received sugar or caffeine along with others who took a placebo.

Coffee can also improve spatial memory. Studies have been done that compared normal coffee drinkers with people who don't drink coffee. When both groups drank coffee, their spatial memory improved greatly. What was more interesting was the people who normally drank coffee didn't receive as many benefits from the coffee as the ones who didn't drink coffee.

Just From Coffee?

A study involving women over 65 who had been diagnosed with cardiovascular disease measured how much coffee they drank and then had them do cognitive assessments regularly over a five-year time span. Results showed women who drank more coffee, did better on cognitive tests.

Energy Drinks

What about young people who drink energy drinks? Energy drinks do contain a lot of caffeine but will it also improve cognitive functions. It will increase alertness but doesn't show any difference in cognitive functions when compared to people who were given a placebo.

Caffeinated Gum?

If you would like another way to get caffeine, instead of drinking coffee, you could chew caffeinated herbal gum. This gum can improve memory just like coffee.

Can Coffee Help Extrovert's Memory?

Are you extroverted? One study shows that working memory can be improved by extroverted adults who drank coffee. Another study tried to replicate its findings. This study found that memory and serial recall in extroverted adults improved when they drank coffee. Coffee also improved their reaction speed and how well they received new information.

Potential Benefits

The average American will consume around 300 mg of caffeine each day. They usually get if from soft drinks, tea, and coffee. Many studies say the caffeine can give health benefits. Coffee could reduce developing liver disease. Other studies say drinking between two and four cups of coffee could reduce the thoughts of suicide.

Cautions

There is some bad news that the stimulant in coffee could disrupt sleep even hours after drinking it. Other studies have shown that caffeine from energy drinks could alter how the heart functions properly.

There has been a lot of research done about coffee and how it can affect cognitive abilities and memory. Results can vary, but there is a general idea that coffee can boost cognitive functions. Some studies say that the way you get caffeine is important since coffee works better than other sources.

Just a word of caution in case you decide to drink cup after cup of coffee. There might be health risks for some people. Even small amounts of caffeine could be detrimental to health.

Gum

Students will try any trick to help them through school. It might be munching on snacks or using mnemonic devices. There are lots of various foods that can help with your memory but can chewing gum help? Many studies have been done on the effects of chewing gum and memory, specifically auditory and visual memory.

Chewing gum causes "mastication-induced arousal." No, it doesn't sound pretty, but it does mean what it sounds like. The repetitive motion when chewing gum increases your blood pressure and gives your cells lots of oxygen. This will help you improve your memory and concentrate better.

Just smelling gum can give your memory a jumpstart. You might have wondered why a specific smell can bring up certain memories. The olfactory bypasses the thalamus. This is the main part that processes sensory information. Signals from the olfactory have a pass directly to the amygdala and hippocampus. These parts are linked to memory and emotions.

People who chew gum while learning could recall and retrieve the information faster than people who don't chew gum. This is all thanks to context-dependent effects. This happens because the brain creates a link with chewing gum and learning and creates a habit. Try to chew gum the next time you have a lecture pop a piece of gum in your mouth. When you have an exam, try chewing gum about ten minutes before to boost your recall. You might be pleasantly surprised at how many answers you know.

Chewing gum can also boost cortisol levels and improve your mood. This, in turn, will increase alertness. When you are alert, you will have a better memory.

Mint smells can specifically enhance memory and cognition by lowering stress, clearing congestion, and increases blood flow. Next time you are standing in line at the store, grab some mint gum. You might begin surprising people with your sharp memory and minty fresh breath.

Bad Habits that Slow Memory and Decrease Productivity

Smoking and Drinking

Smoking and excessive drinking can have negative impacts on memory. The impairment that is associated with using these substances is more than using just one of these. Basically, it is a double whammy.

Research has shown that excessively drinking more than 14 servings in one week plus smoking can cause numerous negative memory and health problems. This means that if you are a man and drink more than eight servings at one time plus you smoke you are doing a lot of damage to your body. For a female, it would be six servings.

Excessively drinking alcohol will damage prospective memory. A group of volunteers was asked to hand a scientist a book after giving a cue or calling a specific number at a certain time: volunteers who binge drank didn't remember to carry out as many actions as a volunteer who didn't drink at all. Similar patterns were also found with people who smoked. People who smoke every day won't carry out as many actions as people who haven't ever smoked.

Drinking to excess and smoking will impair memory if used separately, but when they are used together, it intensifies the effects. Smoking can worsen memories of people who drink alcohol excessively. People who smoke and drink will have more memory problems, won't be able to think fast or effectively, and will have problems solving puzzles. People who are addicted to cigarettes and alcohol will have more brain damage than people who don't. People who are addicted will have a thinning in the frontal cortex. This part of the brain controls memory.

Polydrug Users

Since most people will drink and smoke, the effects were tested to see how what negative effects it had on prospective memory. Four groups of volunteers were tested: a control group that didn't smoke or drink, people who smoke and drank to excess, people who smoke but didn't drink that often, and people who drank to excess but didn't smoke. These volunteers were tested to see if they could remember to do six actions. In three of these the volunteers were asked to do a specific task at a certain time like "In six minutes, you need to pick up the blue pen." The other three the volunteers were asked to do a specific action when given a certain cue like "When you get to a question about cheese, please hand the book to me." They were asked to do these while working on puzzles.

The final analysis showed the people who drank to excess and smoked had more impairment than the other groups. This means that things happen when using these substances that will impact the memory negatively.

This study was the first to show how these substances affect prospective remembering. This is important since it shows prospective memory can be compromised when a person smokes and drinks excessively.

We hope these findings will improve people's understanding of how dangerous smoking and drinking is beyond the normal public warnings about health.

Exercise

There are many great reasons to be active physically. The main ones are reducing the chances of developing diabetes, stroke, and heart disease. You might want to look better, prevent depression, lower your blood pressure, or lose weight. You might be experiencing brain fog that comes as we age. The good news is that exercising can change the way the brain protects its thinking and memory skills.

Researchers have found that doing aerobic exercises regularly, the ones that make you sweat and gets your heart pumping; will give a boost to the hippocampus. This part of the brain helps with learning and verbal memory. Muscle toning, balance, and resistance training won't give you the same results.

This is needed since scientists say one person is diagnosed with dementia every four seconds somewhere in the world. They have estimated that by 2050 there will be more than 115 million people in the world with dementia.

Exercise can help thinking and memory by both indirect and direct ways. The benefits come from the brain's ability to stimulate a chemical that affects how healthy our brain cells are, grow new blood vessels, and even helps new brain cells to survive. The brain can also reduce inflammation and insulin resistance.

Exercising can also improve sleep and mood, along with reducing anxiety and stress. Any problems in any of these areas can cause cognitive impairment.

Many studies have shown that the medial temporal cortex and the prefrontal cortex that controls memory and thinking will be larger in people that exercise when compared to people who don't. If you regularly exercise for six months to a year, you will have more volume in certain regions of the brain.

So, what exactly do you need to do? Begin exercising. There aren't any specific exercises that are better than others. Most of the research looked at walkers. Basically, any form of aerobic exercise that will get your heart pumping will give you the same results.

How long and how often do you need to exercise? Most of the volunteers were asked to walk briskly for one hour two times each week. That totals to 120 minutes of moderate intensity exercise every week. Some recommend that 30 minutes of moderate physical activity for five days each week or around 150 minutes would be best. If that seems to be too hard, begin with ten minutes every day and increase until you get to 30 minutes.

If you don't like walking, think about dancing, squash, tennis, climbing stairs, or swimming. Remember that chores around the house can count, too. Raking leaves, mopping, sweeping, or whatever gets your heart rate up and makes you sweat.

If you don't think you can do this by yourself, try some of these:

- Hire a personal trainer if you are financially able.

- Keep track of your progress to motivate you to get to your goal.

- Find a work out friend or class that holds you accountable.

It doesn't matter what motivates you, just choose an exercise and commit to creating a habit just like remembering to take your medication. As the old saying goes exercise is medicine, and this should be at the top of anybody's list as their number one reason to work out.

Sleep

When talking about the effects on memory, sleep can be a Goldilocks problem meaning that both too little and too much are not good. Try to find the "just right."

Getting a normal amount of sleep around seven hours a night might help maintain memory later on in life. Sleep therapy needs to be looked at to help prevent mental impairment.

A group of volunteers took part in a Nurse's Health Study and were asked to keep track of their sleep habits in 1986 and 2000. These people were interviewed about their thinking skills and memory three times within a six-year period. Researchers say that people who only slept five or fewer hours each night or slept longer than nine hours had worse performance as compared to people who got around seven or eight hours of sleep. Researchers said that people who either overslept or underslept were two years older mentally than people who got around seven or eight hours each night.

Beyond Memory

One study could actually prove that getting too much or little sleep causes thinking or memory problems. This is in line with other studies showing the harmful effects of poor sleep habits. Some research has shown that poor sleep can lead to depression, type 2 diabetes, stroke, and heart disease.

How does sleep affect memory? People that are sleep deprived could have narrowed blood vessels, diabetes, and high blood pressure. Any of these could decrease blood flow in the brain. The cells of the brain need plenty of sugar and oxygen so when there is a problem with blood flow it will affect the brain's ability to function the right way.

Poor sleep can affect the brain in other ways. When the brain is sleep deprived, it can cause deposits of beta-amyloid to build up. Beta-amyloid is a protein that can cause a decline in thinking and memory and increases the risk of developing dementia.

What if you get too much sleep? If you get more than ten hours of sleep each night, often have poor sleep quality. The most important numbers might not be how much sleep but the quality of sleep you are getting.

Another possibility is the two way street between memory and sleep: the quality of sleep can affect thinking and memory along with the changes in the brain that causes thinking, and memory problems could disrupt sleep.

Better Sleep

Here are some tips to help you get a better quality of sleep:

- Create a relaxing bedtime routine along with a specific time: listen to calming music or take a warm bubble bath.

- Use the bed for lovemaking or sleeping. Don't watch television or read in bed.

- Make sure your bedroom is quiet and dark and your bed is comfy. You could use earplugs or a sleep mask if you need to.

- If you aren't asleep in 20 minutes, get out of bed and go to a different room. Find something that relaxes you. Never get turn on your tablet, computer, or television. Once you begin to feel sleepy, go back to bed. Never delay your wake-up time to try and make up any sleep that was lost.

- Stay away from alcohol after dinner. Many people think it is a sedative, but it can affect your quality sleep.

- Exercise. Try to get around 30 minutes of moderate exercise each day. Try to do this early in the day. Try doing some yoga or stretches to help relax your mind and muscles close to bedtime.

- To keep from having to use the bathroom a lot during the night, avoid any fluids after dinner.

- When you can do any demanding or stressful tasks early in your day and less demanding activities later. This can help you wind down after a hard day.

- Limit your caffeine intake and don't drink any after 2 pm.

- Never go to bed hungry and never eat a large meal just before going to bed. If you need a snack, make sure it is light and bland.

Try to practice relaxed breathing. Use slow breaths when exhaling.

Conclusion

Thanks for making it through to the end of *Memory and Accelerated Learning*. Let's hope it was informative and able to provide you with all of the tools you need to achieve your goals whatever they may be.

Remember learning and memory can be improved and increased through simple action steps. It's not static. It's growing and changing your entire life. Increased learning ability will help you to learn more things with ease and less frustration. When coupled with improved memory, you will be amazed at the things you will be able to achieve. Think about learning a new language. How easy would it be with better memory? You would be less likely to give up when things get hard.

First things first, though, you have to make sure that you maintain a single focus. Multi-tasking is a myth that people think they have mastered. Your mind is only able to focus on a single task at a time, and jumping around from task to task isn't getting anything done faster. All you will end up feeling is frustrated. Figure out the one thing that you need to focus on, and work on it until it is finished.

When it comes to memory, don't forget that the more senses you involve in remembering something, the easier it will be to remember it when the time comes. Create a mental picture that you would never be able to forget. Make it as crazy as you possibly can.

Don't think that imagination is something that only children can use. Imagination has always been, and will always be, a very powerful skill in anything and everything that you do. It helps you remember and learn things. That's why teachers will use pictures alongside information to help people remember what they are learning. Images are powerful tools for the human mind, and so often, people forget their power.

Besides learning how to use a mental image and your imagination, you can also create mind maps. These are not only

84

helpful for learning, but they are also fun to make. The simple rote method of learning has failed people for far too long. Mind mapping is the new way to remember and learn things, so use it and reap its amazing benefits.

Remember that increasing your reading speed is another viable option is accelerating your learning. You will not only be able to learn more in a shorter amount of time, but you will also retain more information. Now, keep in mind, you don't have to use speed reading all the time, and there are times when you shouldn't speed read. If you are reading for fun, then there is really no need for speed reading. Also, if it's an important work document that you have to thoroughly go over and present something on it, then it is best to not speed read either. The main thing is to make sure that you use these skills you have learned at the right time.

When it comes down to it, though, if you can't maintain your memories, what good are they? Once you have grasped the ability to increase your learning and improve your memory, the time has come to make sure you don't forget those things. This is probably the most overlooked part of the learning process. People think once they have learned something that it will always be there when they need. While in some cases this may be true, it's not always true for everybody.

If you don't access and use the information you have learned from time to time, it will leave you. You've heard the saying, if you don't use it, you'll lose it. Well, that's how memories work. If you don't have to use a memory, then just look back over it from time to time. When you learn a new language, you don't just read the words in a book. You speak them out loud. While you may not be around another person that speaks that language, you can still speak it just for fun. This will make sure that you remember the language when the time comes for you to use it.

Lastly, you have to make sure that you give up the habit of procrastination. Sure, it's super easy to do. Why else would so many people cause themselves distress if it wasn't? Everybody does, but very few try to stop it. Some allow it to affect their lives so much that it affects their jobs and relationships. Nobody wants to hear the words, "You're fired," but that's exactly where severe procrastination can lead you. Do whatever it is that you have to do to make sure that you get rid of procrastination and turn it into productivity. Remember, this doesn't have to mean that you are mean to yourself and force yourself to work endlessly. This can be fun where you schedule yourself some procrastination breaks.

The important thing in all of this is to go easy on yourself. Everything that you have learned can improve your life, but it will take time and effort on your part. Take it slow, and remember that you can achieve a better memory and learning ability. It will happen. Kicking those other bad habits will help as well. While that may be easier said than done, it's important to your mind. As you have learned, excessive smoking and drinking don't serve you in any way. Lack of sleep and exercise also hurts your mind, both of which can be easily remedied.

Baby steps are what will get you where you need to be. Leaps and bounds will leave you frustrated, and you will probably give up. Nothing happens overnight, so make sure that you go at your own speed.

Get started using these techniques that you have learned. You will be amazed at what you can accomplish in life. Before you know it, you will have learned a new language, another habit, a musical instrument, whatever your heart desires.

Finally, if you found this useful in any way, a review on Amazon is always appreciated!

CPSIA information can be obtained
at www.ICGtesting.com
Printed in the USA
LVHW012038180520
655843LV00006B/621